Aligning Hearts and Accounts

A Path to Financial Intimacy for Couples

Strengthen your relationship by creating harmony and mastering your money together.

by Grace Del Rey

The Saving Grace Money Method

Aligning Hearts and Accounts is a work of my own creation.

The information in this book was correct at the time of publication, and the Author does not assume any liability for loss or damage caused by errors or omissions, again, this is my perspective, opinion, and experience, so it has been written as such.

Copyright © 2024 by Grace Del Rey

All rights reserved.

No part of this book may be reproduced or transmitted in any form or by any means, electronic or mechanical, including photocopying, recording, or by any information and retrieval systems, without the written permission of the Publisher, except where permitted by law.

ISBN - 978-1-961185-60-9

www.inomniaparatuspublishing.com

Welcome to 'Aligning Hearts and Accounts: A Path to Financial Intimacy for Couples.' I hope this book beckons you to deepen your bond by exploring your financial landscape together. Through navigating your finances together you build the foundation to trust each other in aligning your dreams, values, and goals inside a doable financial framework.

This book will serve as a guide and companion on your path to financial intimacy. It will help you strengthen your relationship by creating harmony and mastering your money together.

In the following pages, you will discover prompts, exercises, and pages that encourage open and honest conversations about money—a topic that can significantly enrich a relationship when shared.

It's not just about numbers and budgets; it's about understanding each other's financial histories, aspirations, and fears and creating an exciting future that reflects both of your dreams.

I invite you to explore the idea that financial planning is not a source of stress but a source of strength. Everything has been created to bring you closer, assist in building a foundation of trust and mutual respect, and build a life of healthy communication that extends far beyond your finances.

By engaging with this book, you embark on a proactive path to avoid the pitfalls that financial misunderstandings can bring. Together, you'll celebrate achievements, navigate setbacks, and continually evolve toward a shared vision of prosperity for your future.

Aligning Hearts and Accounts is more than a book; it's a gateway to a deeper, more connected partnership where financial harmony is just the beginning.

I am honored to take you on a shared adventure where mastering your money becomes a powerful way to strengthen your love.

♡ Grace

Introduction

This book was born from the concept of my two businesses. I founded SGBS Consulting Inc., an accounting firm I have managed over the past thirty years. In addition, I recently formed a dynamic partnership in a property that houses a wedding/event venue and a glamping experience.

One of the first significant investments a couple makes is getting married. Whether it's $500 or $100,000 for a wedding, it's the first big event a couple will decide on. Regardless if the money for the wedding comes from your account, your parent, or a relative, these funds are directed toward a shared experience you desire to create in your reality. It's an excellent opportunity to establish a level of understanding of how to best communicate on challenging subjects like money.

My accounting firm works with all kinds of businesses. We set up operations systems to account for money flow, create budgets and partnerships, and forecast the future of the various companies.

With all the many ways to communicate in the world, I noticed that creating the time to have a deeper conversation can be challenging. However, these deeper conversations are where self-reflection can profoundly impact one's future endeavors.

What do I mean by a deeper conversation? Ask each other more questions and be honest and vulnerable when sharing your truth or beliefs. Hold space for each other to heal from prior experiences with money and relationships. Support each other with trying on new beliefs or experimenting and redefining your relationship with money if you adopt a belief that no longer serves you.

For example, my parents came from very different backgrounds. My father was born into a farmer's life and was raised in a cement house with dirt floors. He'd wake up at dawn to milk the cows and clean the pig pens before walking to school. Conversely, my mother was born into a wealthy family where she had cooks, butlers, drivers, and maids, and higher education was a given.

Besides the dramatic differences in my parents' upbringing, they came from two different cultures. My mother is Chinese and came to the United States to go to college, whereas my father was a true blue-redneck American. They both said they loved going to the beach. There's a distinction when they both said I love going to the beach. My mom loves sitting on the beach watching the waves, whereas my father loves sailing a sailboat in the ocean, two very different beach experiences.

The same is true with money. I created this book to help couples have deeper conversations about their relationship with money individually and as a couple. Many marriages end in divorce due to financial problems, conflict, and arguments. The longevity of marriage will depend on the couple's ability to develop their communication and connection skills on deeper levels.

Establishing a solid connection and safe environment as a couple can lay the foundation to align your joint financial goals. It may seem silly to clarify what it means to have money in the bank. For example, some people feel comfortable with having a dollar in the bank. That, to them, means they are ahead of the curve. In contrast, others may see having only a dollar in the bank as being broke.

Using my parents as an example, my father felt we were living well because my parents were jointly able to pay for the condo we lived in, put food on the table, go to the beach for a week in the summer, and pay for a few extras. The fact that we lived in a three-bedroom house with four children did not phase my father. Whereas my mother envisioned each child having their own bedroom, paying for our higher education and more extras. My mother was able to manifest her dream twice over in having two houses that each had 5 to 6 bedrooms. However, she accomplished these dreams alone as my father didn't want to take on more responsibilities with a bigger house as he grew closer to retirement age.

This book is to help you as a couple clarify your language, examine the details of what it means to have money in the bank, in savings, etc., and compromise if you have extremes in what is comfortable for you and the family you are creating. Establish what is important to you both as a couple and learn how best to talk to each other about concerns that come up before they turn into arguments and resentments.

The Connection Series

Below is a QR code that unlocks essential resources designed to help you with your experience. The Connection Series offers various links to exercises, excel tables, and prompts to fortify your bond and ensure a safe space for both partners to grow together.

Before you dive in, I would like you to explore these tools. The first link is to a grounding meditation, which provides a calm starting point and helps you center your thoughts and emotions and be present with yourself and your partner.

The second directs you to a connection exercise crafted to deepen your bond, facilitating a closer, more intimate understanding of each other. There are many more exercises and downloadable worksheets for you to use as you go through the book.

Throughout the book, I have included the QR code where an exercise or worksheet might be helpful.

These resources are tailored to ensure you both start on solid ground, ready to explore and grow together with clarity and connection.

In addition to these, there is a toolbox of resources in the back of this journal that will be referred to throughout the journey. The more you use the resources and do the exercises, the more you will get out of them.

Before We Get Started...

Before diving into the heart of this journey, it's crucial to establish a foundation of trust and respect. We want to foster financial intimacy, but its effectiveness is rooted in the way you communicate and navigate through the process together. For success, setting boundaries and guidelines from the outset is paramount.

A pivotal tool in this process is establishing a "safe word." This might seem unconventional in the context of financial planning, but it's a powerful way to maintain a supportive and pressure-free environment.

The safe word or phrase acts as a mutual agreement; a respectful signal that either partner can use when discussions feel overwhelming or emotions run high. It's a pause button, allowing both of you to step back, breathe, and approach the topic with renewed clarity and understanding at a later time.

Establishing this safe word from the beginning also acknowledges that while our journey toward financial intimacy aims to bring us closer, the path may sometimes be challenging. Conversations about money can unearth deep-seated fears, past experiences, and vulnerabilities. This acts as your commitment to each other that these conversations, though difficult and emotional, will always be approached with care, compassion, and mutual respect.

In addition to the safe word, setting clear boundaries and guidelines about how and when you will engage in these financial conversations is equally important. Deciding on regular check-ins, respecting each other's perspectives, and committing to honesty and openness sets the stage for a productive and empowering experience.

Remember, the goal of this book is not just to align your accounts but to strengthen your bond by tackling your financial future as a team.

By establishing these foundational rules, you're not just preparing to grow your finances; you're fortifying your relationship, ensuring it's strong, resilient, and deeply connected for years to come.

Safe Word or Phrase

Examples: I'm done, I need a break, Pineapple...

_____
_____
_____
_____

Additional Rules and Guidelines for the Conversation

Examples: Always do the "I see you" exercise before starting, or if emotionally charged try hugging each other for 5 minutes without talking. Never start a discussion when extremely tired. Please don't use anything shared in a session in a future fight. Remember, we are doing are best and have patience with yourself and your partner.

_____
_____
_____
_____
_____
_____

Setting The Expectations

Independently write out what you as individuals hope to achieve and understand about each other with this journal.

Partner 1	Partner 2

Let's Get Started!

Now that we have covered some basics, it is time to begin this transformative journey! You've taken a brave step towards aligning your finances and deepening your connection as a couple.

This journey you're starting is much more than numbers on a page; it's about building a future that reflects both of your dreams, values, and aspirations. Doing this as a team amplifies its power, bringing you closer and strengthening your bond through shared goals and mutual support.

As you navigate this process, remember that you are each other's greatest ally and support system. Some of the exercises may be challenging, and some of the prompts may cause painful memories. Face them together, support each other, hold each other up through the tricky parts, and celebrate the wins as a team.

The insights, plans, and dreams you share on these pages are the building blocks of your shared future. Approaching each step with open hearts and minds, you'll discover that financial intimacy is a profound way to express love and commitment.

Welcome to a journey of growth, understanding, and a deeper connection, where you craft your finances, life, and future together.

Chapter 1

Setting the Stage: Understanding Your Financial Histories

Section 1
Reflecting on Individual Money Stories

In this section, we're driving down childhood memory lane to see how your past experiences with money from childhood have shaped your beliefs around money today. Everything that has happened in your life up until now impacts you, even if you don't realize it.

Understanding each other's money history allows you a glimpse of the path you each experienced up to now. As you tackle your childhood experience with money together, you will develop trust and compassion as you plan your future.

Keep in mind, some of this could be emotionally challenging. If you have not already established your safe word or set boundaries, you should do it now prior to getting started.

Using the prompts below, answer the questions and journal on the experiences. Each partner should do this independently before coming together for a discussion.

Money Story Prompts

As you reflect on your earliest memory related to money, please allow yourself to become the observer of the memory. Try not to engage in the emotion of the memory, but rather as if you are watching a movie and can take in all the players and where they are coming from at that particular moment in the movie.

Was it a specific event, a conversation, or perhaps an observation? Could you describe the scene and your feelings associated with the experience?

Please think back to how money was discussed in your family. Was it an open topic, or was it shrouded in secrecy? Share how this communication style shaped your views on money.

When did you first realize you needed money as a child? Did your parents constantly say things about money, like " Money doesn't grow on trees" Or "You have to work hard to make money?" Did you see your parents work hard to earn money or make sacrifices for the betterment of the family? Did your family take vacations and discuss a budget? Did your parents or guardians have credit card debt? Did your parents have savings and talk to you about savings or investments?

Analyze how the impact of your early experiences with money has shaped your current financial habits. How have those initial impressions influenced your spending, saving, and financial planning today?

Partner 1 Reflections

Partner 2 Reflections

Chapter 1 Section 1 Discussion Prompts ♡

Before you start the discussion prompts, please do the "I see you" exercise from the Connected Series.

- Discuss any similarities or differences you noticed. How do you think these early experiences have shaped your individual attitudes towards money now?

- Reflecting on how money was discussed in your families, what patterns do you observe? How might these patterns influence how you manage money together as a couple?

- Discuss the impact of your past financial experiences on your current relationship. Are there any habits or beliefs you've brought into your relationship that you might want to change or strengthen?

- Let's talk about any fears or anxieties you have around money that may be rooted in your past. How can you support each other in overcoming these fears to build a healthier financial future together?

- Considering your financial habits and attitudes, where do you see potential for conflict, and where do you see opportunities for growth? How can you both use your differences to complement each other and strengthen your financial unity?

Discussion Notes

Section 2
Identifying Financial Traumas and Triumphs

Let's dive into your past money milestones and obstacles to see how they shape your financial actions and mindset today. It's all about understanding the journey from then to now and its influence on your money choices.

Creating Individual Lists of Impactful Financial Events

Each partner will list significant financial traumas (e.g., a family bankruptcy, job loss, lawsuit, theft) and triumphs (e.g., paying off debt, receiving an inheritance, being awarded a dream contract or job) they've experienced.

The list does not only have to be things that have happened to you as a person, it could also be things you have watched your parents or other influential people in your life experience.

Partner 1

Partner 2

Chapter 1 Section 2 Discussion Prompts

Before you start the discussion prompts, please do the grounding meditation from the Connected Series.

Let's share the financial traumas and triumphs you have both listed. How have these experiences affected our views on risk, security, and financial planning?

Discussing your personal and observed financial traumas, how do these past events influence your current financial behaviors? Are there any patterns you wish to change?

Reflect on the triumphs you've experienced or witnessed. What lessons did these victories teach you about managing finances, and how can you apply them to your shared financial goals?

How do your individual experiences with financial trauma and triumph complement each other? Where can you find strength in your combined histories to face future financial challenges?

In light of understanding each other's financial traumas and triumphs, how can you better support one another in healing from past hurts and celebrating successes together? What steps can you take to build a resilient financial future as a team?

Discussion Notes

_____
_____
_____
_____
_____
_____
_____
_____
_____
_____
_____
_____
_____
_____
_____
_____
_____
_____
_____

Section 3
Using Financial History to Shape Your Future

This section is about opening up and exploring each other's financial highs and lows, and the lessons we've picked up along the way. It's a chance to really get each other's perspectives on money, understanding our individual paths to make our collective journey stronger.

It is also about learning to dream together and to appreciate the differences in your experiences and using that to lean on each others strengths to build your future as a team.

Joint Timeline Creation

Now that you understand your financial history, it is time to put that information to use. What pieces do you want to keep, what perspectives do you want to change, and how can you use that information to create a timeline of goals and milestones?

Write out a few financial goals in the boxes on the next page. Feel free to add your own in the blank boxes.

As you identify the goals, reframe for the moment on "THE HOW" you all will obtain your goals. Instead, I encourage you to focus on what you, as a couple, would like to create and experience together.

In another section, we will break down the how and the timeline. But for now, I ask that you let yourselves dream and emotionally experience how good it feels to create what's possible.

Click the QR Code to do a guided meditation, Visualizing Your Future.

1 week from now...	1 month from now...
2 months from now...	3 months from now...
6 months from now...	12 months from now

2 years from now...	What will our first big expense as a couple be?
When do we want to buy our first house together? How big?	Are we going to have children? When are we going to have children?
At what age do we want to retire?	How often do we want to go on vacation?

Chapter 1 Section 3 Discussion Prompts

"Money firsts" conversation starters: Engage in dialogues about each other's first job, first big purchase, first investment, etc., to uncover values, fears, and aspirations related to money.

How do our past financial experiences shape our future financial dreams? Let's identify where our visions align and where they diverge, exploring how we can support each other's dreams.

Reflecting on our financial histories, what are the key lessons we've learned that influence our future aspirations? Let's discuss how these insights can help us build a united financial path.

In what ways do our past financial experiences inform our individual and collective attitudes towards risk, savings, and investment for our future? Let's explore areas of alignment and difference to better understand each other.

Considering our financial pasts, how do we envision our financial future together? Let's discuss how our shared and individual dreams can merge into a cohesive plan, recognizing and respecting our differences.

Discussion Notes

Chapter 2

Creating a Common Financial Language

Section 1
Defining Key Financial Terms Together

This section provides a comprehensive glossary of financial terms and concepts that couples may encounter in their financial journey.

The goal is to ensure both partners understand these terms mutually, fostering a common language for discussing finances.

In the next few pages, you will review financial terms and consider how they apply to you, how they relate to you individually and as a couple, and what you both envision for your lives.

What does it mean to be FINANCIALLY STABLE? Does that mean you have enough money each week, month, or year to cover your living costs? Or does that mean you have six months of emergency funds in savings to cover you if you or your partner are sick, out of work, or having to take care of a family member, which prevents them from working?

Understanding your NET WORTH is a powerful tool for taking control of your financial situation. Net Worth is calculated by subtracting your liabilities from your assets. Assets can be anything from cash in your bank account to property you own like your home and car, your book of business, and investments. On the other hand, liabilities are credit card and loan debts—basically, any money you owe.

If you have significant debt, your net worth may be negative. However, this situation is temporary. When considering what net worth means to you, envision the financial position you aspire to and take steps towards achieving it.

You might have heard there is no such thing as GOOD DEBT. But if you start a business, you might have to use your credit cards to help finance business start-up costs to get you going. If you use this strategy, please plan how to pay the "good debt" off, whether applying for an SBA loan or first money back, etc.

BAD DEBT is really bad. And you are not horrible for having it. However, bad debt is like eating junk food. You bought clothes you didn't need or went out to eat more than you needed to and spent money you didn't have. If you did that in the past, this is the time to think about how you plan to be more responsible in your spending, whether you are indulging yourself or your loved ones. Think about how you both want to approach it with each other.

Lastly, BUDGETING isn't a bad word. Budgeting is an opportunity to connect your financial present with your financial future. It's a tool that empowers you to make intentional decisions about where your money goes, ensuring that it aligns with your priorities and goals. By understanding your net worth and distinguishing between good and bad debt, you can create a budget that reflects your values and aspirations. Remember, budgeting isn't about restriction; it's about liberation—the freedom to live the life you want, both now and in the years to come.

Financial Stability: _____
_____
_____

Net-Worth: _____
_____
_____

Good Debt: _____
_____
_____

Bad Debt: _____
_____
_____

Budgeting: _____
_____
_____

Insert Your Own: <_____>
_____
_____
_____

Insert Your Own: <_____>
_____
_____
_____

Chapter 2 Section 1 Discussion Prompts

Share what 'financial security' means to each of you. How can we work together to achieve that feeling in our relationship? What would that look like in reality? How much is in the joint account? How much in savings, retirement, and investments? How much money ideally is flowing in each month?

How do we define 'unnecessary expenses'? Let's share our views and find common ground on what we consider essential versus optional. Please review without judgment. For example, you may have essential expenses such as having your roots colored, but you don't have to go out for dinner that week to counterbalance that week's budget.

Share your 'savings philosophy'? How much do we aim to save, and what are we saving for? Let's align our savings goals.

Let's explore our thoughts on 'investing for the future.' What types of investments make us comfortable, and how can we balance risk and reward together?

How do we feel about 'debt management'? Let's share our strategies for handling debt and discuss how we can support each other in becoming debt-free.

Section 2
Establishing Shared Financial Goals and Values

In this section, you will be guided through exercises to identify and articulate individual and joint financial goals, values, and priorities.

We will build off Chapter 1, Section 3 to create more specific goals and begin to create action steps to achieve them.

We will also dive into deeper discussion to aid in the understanding of the difference between wants and needs, and aligning financial objectives with personal values for both partners.

Defining Core Financial Values

Each partner should write out a list of their financial priorities and why they are essential. The goal is to establish an understanding of your values individually and together.

This will be the base from which you set goals as a couple.

Examples: being debt-free, living in a lovely house, owning a home, driving a new car, investing for retirement, having savings, having an entertainment fund, traveling, etc.

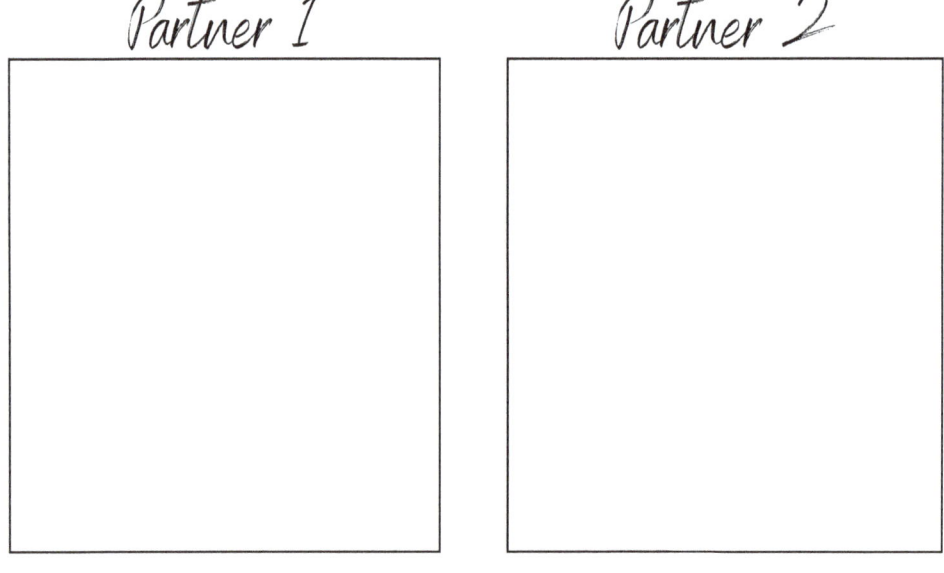

Detailed Goal Setting

Partner 1: Use the following template to plan your financial goals for the next 12 months. The toolbox has additional pages.

Goal 1:

Specific — What do we want to accomplish and why?

Measurable — How will we know when we have accomplished it?

Achievable — How can we accomplish this goal?

Relevant — Is this the right time for us to be working towards this goal?

Timebound — When do we want to accomplish this goal by?

Goal 2:

Specific.

Measurable.

Achievable.

Relevant.

Timebound.

Goal 3:

Specific.

Measurable.

Achievable.

Relevant.

Timebound.

Detailed Goal Setting

Partner 2: Use the following template to plan your financial goals for the next 12 months. The toolbox has additional pages.

Goal 1:

Specific — What do we want to accomplish and why?

Measurable — How will we know when we have accomplished it?

Achievable — How can we accomplish this goal?

Relevant — Is this the right time for us to be working towards this goal?

Timebound — When do we want to accomplish this goal by?

Goal 2:

Specific.

Measurable.

Achievable.

Relevant.

Timebound.

Goal 3:

Specific.

Measurable.

Achievable.

Relevant.

Timebound.

Detailed Goal Setting

Couple: Use the following template to plan your financial goals for the next 12 months. The toolbox has additional pages.

Goal 1:

Specific — What do we want to accomplish and why?

Measurable — How will we know when we have accomplished it?

Achievable — How can we accomplish this goal?

Relevant — Is this the right time for us to be working towards this goal?

Timebound — When do we want to accomplish this goal by?

Goal 2:

Specific.

Measurable.

Achievable.

Relevant.

Timebound.

Goal 3:

Specific.

Measurable.

Achievable.

Relevant.

Timebound.

Goal Tracker - Partner 1

Keep track of your goals and your progress. Additional pages available in the toolbox.

Goal 1:

Start Date

End Date

My Why

Action Steps
- ○
- ○
- ○
- ○

Notes

Goal 2:

Start Date

End Date

My Why

Action Steps
- ○
- ○
- ○
- ○

Notes

Goal 3:

Start Date

End Date

My Why

Action Steps
- ○
- ○
- ○
- ○

Notes

Goal Tracker - Partner 2

Keep track of your goals and your progress. Additional pages available in the toolbox.

Goal 1:

Start Date

End Date

My Why

Action Steps
- ○
- ○
- ○
- ○

Notes

Goal 2:

Start Date

End Date

My Why

Action Steps
- ○
- ○
- ○
- ○

Notes

Goal 3:

Start Date

End Date

My Why

Action Steps
- ○
- ○
- ○
- ○

Notes

Goal Tracker - Couple

Keep track of your goals and your progress. Additional pages available in the toolbox.

Goal 1:

Start Date
End Date
My Why

Action Steps
○
○
○
○

Notes

Goal 2:

Start Date
End Date
My Why

Action Steps
○
○
○
○

Notes

Goal 3:

Start Date
End Date
My Why

Action Steps
○
○
○
○

Notes

Chapter 2 Section 2 Discussion Prompts

 Let's each share one personal financial goal and one we have for us as a couple. How do these reflect our values and priorities?

 How do we prioritize spending in areas like travel, home improvements, or education? Let's discuss what matters most to us and align our budget.

 What are our long-term financial aspirations? Let's articulate where we see ourselves in one month, three months, six months, and one year. You can jump to five, ten, and twenty years. However, start with where you want to be in a year, then track backward to where you will need to be in one month to be on track. And how we can work together to get there. - See QR Code for meditation that walks you through the process

 In what ways do our individual spending habits impact our joint financial health? Let's discuss any adjustments we might consider to support our shared goals.

 How do we approach financial decision-making when our values or priorities differ? Let's create a strategy for navigating these discussions with understanding and respect.

Section 3
Dialogue Prompts to Facilitate Understanding and Empathy

This section is designed to deepen the emotional and practical understanding of each partner's financial perspective through guided dialogue prompts.

Things are not going to always go as planned. It is important to establish a communication style that allows for dealing with challenging scenarios.

The objective is to build empathy, reduce financial stress, and strengthen the couple's ability to navigate financial discussions with compassion and empathy.

Chapter 2 Section 3 Discussion Prompts

- When financial stress arises, how do we each tend to react emotionally? Sharing our feelings might help us understand each other better and find a supportive approach.

- Can we recall a past financial challenge we faced together? Let's discuss how we handled it, what we learned, and how it can inform our future decisions.

- Let's each share a fear we have regarding our finances. Understanding these can help us support each other and build a stronger financial foundation together.

- How can we create a safe space for discussing finances, especially when we disagree? Establishing rules for respectful communication can help us tackle tough topics.

- What steps can we take to ensure we're both involved and informed about our financial decisions? Being on the same page can reduce stress and build trust.

Discussion Notes

Chapter 3

Financial Planning as a Couple

Section 1: Assessing Current Financial Health: Income, Debt, Savings, and Investments

This section equips couples with tools to evaluate their current financial situation comprehensively.

It involves exercises to calculate combined income, total debt (including credit cards, student loans, and mortgages), savings in emergency funds or other accounts, and existing investments.

Example Accounts

Use the table below to write out the balances of all of your accounts, including debt, checking and savings accounts.

DATE	DESCRIPTION	ACCT TYPE	AMOUNT
5/2/2024	Personal - Credit Union	Checking	$ 5,534
5/2/2024	Personal -- Live Oak	Savings	$ 25,500
5/2/2024	Personal -- Ameriprise	Investment	$ 175,000
5/2/2024	Total Asset		$ 206,034
5/2/2024	Personal -- Chase	Credit Card	$ 5,500
5/2/2024	Personal -- Amex	Credit Card	$ 15,500
5/2/2024	Student Loan	Loan	$34,000
5/2/2024	Car Loan	Loan	$25,000
5/2/2024	Total Liability		$74,500
5/2/2024	Total Net Worth		$ 131,534

Partner 1 Accounts

Use the table below to write out the balances of all of your accounts, including debt, checking and savings accounts.

DATE	DESCRIPTION	ACCT TYPE	AMOUNT

Partner 2 Accounts

Use the table below to write out the balances of all of your accounts, including debt, checking and savings accounts.

DATE	DESCRIPTION	ACCT TYPE	AMOUNT

Joint Accounts

Use the table below to write out the balances of all of your joint accounts, including debt, checking and savings accounts.

DATE	DESCRIPTION	ACCT TYPE	AMOUNT

Net Worth Calculator

Add your total assets, subtract the total liabilities (debts) to get the networht of each partner as an individual and together.

Partner One Account Totals	
Total Liquid Assets	
Total Liabilities	
Net Worth	

Partner Two Account Totals	
Total Liquid Assets	
Total Liabilities	
Net Worth	

Total of all Accounts	
Total Liquid Assets	
Total Liabilities	
Net Worth	

Chapter 3 Section 1 Discussion Prompts

- Talk about current debts and how you feel about them. Understanding your combined debts can help us make a plan to tackle them together.

- Define financial success from each partner's perspective and explore where net worth fits into their shared vision. This exercise helps align their financial goals.

- Explore strategies to reduce debt, such as debt consolidation or making extra payments. Identifying mutual strategies will pave the way for a unified financial approach.

- Determine areas of focus for building net worth, including investments, savings, or debt reduction. Prioritizing these areas will help them set achievable financial targets together.

- Examine how each partner views the role of debt in achieving their dreams, such as home ownership or entrepreneurship. Understanding these perspectives is crucial for their financial planning.

Discussion Notes

Section 2: Budgeting Together: Needs vs. Wants

Here, we will focus on the difference between essential expenses (needs) and non-essential expenses (wants) through interactive budgeting exercises.

This part of the workbook introduces the concept of creating a joint budget that aligns with shared financial goals and values, incorporating both partners' income and expenditure.

Activities include categorizing expenses, setting limits for discretionary spending, and finding ways to reduce costs without compromising quality of life.

The aim is to foster a collaborative approach to managing daily finances and discretionary spending.

Now, it's time to consolidate everything we've learned about each other and our finances, along with the budgeting resources available through the QR code below. Let's weave in the insights from our discussion on priorities and values as we craft our budget. This process entails open dialogue about each category, ensuring that our budget reflects our spending and saving habits and serves as a roadmap towards achieving our goals.

This budget isn't just about numbers; it reflects our shared aspirations and commitments. Let's use it to guide our financial decisions and stay aligned with our vision for the future.

Chapter 3 Section 2 Discussion Prompts

- Identify and list all sources of income for both partners, ensuring a comprehensive understanding of their combined financial resources for budgeting purposes.

- Discuss monthly expenses, separating them into fixed and variable categories, to grasp where the money is currently being allocated and where adjustments might be necessary.

- Set aside time to outline financial priorities, including savings, debt repayment, and lifestyle choices, to ensure the budget aligns with both partners' values and goals.

- Explore discretionary spending habits, focusing on areas such as dining out, entertainment, and hobbies, to find a balance that satisfies both partners without compromising the budget.

- Consider the implementation of a financial cushion within the budget for unexpected expenses, ensuring they maintain financial stability while enjoying their chosen lifestyle.

Discussion Notes

Section 3: Goal Evaluation

In the last section, we crafted an official budget, a crucial step in our financial journey. Now, it's imperative to assess the goals we've set and ensure they harmonize with our actual financial situation.

Alignment between our financial aspirations and our lifestyle is paramount. The budget serves as a roadmap toward our goals, but it's equally vital to monitor cash flow to meet our obligations while maintaining a fulfilling lifestyle.

Striking a balance is key. Being overly restrictive can breed stress, hindering the flow of money to us, while being too lax leaves us adrift without clear financial goals. Finding equilibrium and alignment paves the way for a sustainable financial plan—one that we can adhere to with confidence.

Diving Deeper

As you review your goals and budget, allow yourselves to make adjustments. For example, do you need to make smaller goals with shorter timelines to ensure success? (I.E., How much do you need to save every month to buy a house)

When you go through the budget, are both partners' values and priorities clearly represented?

What changes do you need to make to your budget to reflect your goals, priorities, and values?

What adjustments must you make to your goals or timeline to set yourselves up for success?

Chapter 3 Section 3 Discussion Prompts

- Examine both partners' financial goals and values to identify commonalities and differences, facilitating a deeper understanding and alignment in their financial journey. Be open to what is possible for each other individually and as a couple.

- Reflect on how each partner's individual goals and values are represented within the current budget, and discuss any adjustments needed to ensure you both feel your priorities are adequately addressed.

- Assess the impact of your combined budget on achieving short-term and long-term financial objectives, encouraging adjustments to better support shared goals.

- Encourage an open conversation about the compromises you both might need to make to align your budget with your mutual financial goals and values.

- Initiate a discussion on establishing regular check-ins to revisit and adjust your financial goals, values, and budget as your relationship and financial situation evolve over time.

Discussion Notes

Chapter 4

Navigating Financial Conflicts

Section 1
Identifying Common Triggers for Financial Disagreements

In this section, both partners will engage in individual reflection before coming together for a joint discussion. It's also important to revisit the safe words and boundaries established at the outset of this journal to ensure a supportive and respectful environment.

Embrace any discomfort that arises during these exercises—it's a natural part of growth. Proceed through discussions at a pace that feels comfortable for both of you, allowing ample time for reflection and active listening.

Drawing from Don Miguel Ruiz's "The Four Agreements," strive to embody these principles: be impeccable with your word, avoid taking things personally, refrain from making assumptions, and always do your best. Practicing these agreements fosters present and mindful communication with your partner.

Additionally, take a moment to check in with your body for any tension and engage in the "I see you" exercise together. Recognize that what may seem effortless for one partner can be overwhelming for the other. Use this opportunity to refine communication strategies and strengthen your bond as you navigate challenges together.

Exercise: Identifying triggers and develop strategies to move through them in a supportive and loving way.

Individual Reflection: Each partner spends some time reflecting on past financial disagreements. Identify specific instances, note what triggered the disagreement, and how it made you feel. Be honest and introspective in your reflections.

Joint Session: Come together and share your findings with each other. Listen attentively and without judgment as your partner shares their triggers and feelings. This is a great opportunity to practice not taking anything personal when actively listening to your partner

Create a Trigger Map: Using a piece of paper or a digital tool, collaboratively create a "Trigger Map". List down the triggers identified by both partners. Next to each trigger, categorize them into common themes such as spending habits, financial priorities, communication breakdowns, projections of old hurts, etc.

Develop Strategies: For each trigger or theme on your map, discuss and jot down strategies that could help mitigate these triggers in the future. Strategies might include setting a monthly budget meeting, creating a shared savings goal, or using "I feel" statements when discussing money.

Commitment to Action: Conclude the exercise by selecting one strategy to implement immediately. Commit to a plan on how and when you will put this strategy into action. Schedule a follow-up session to discuss progress and adjust the approach as needed.

Partner 1 Reflection

Partner 2 Reflection

Trigger Map

Create a list of trigger categories to be referenced later. You may add to the list as you move through the other parts of this exercise. If you feel stuck, move on and come back.

_____

_____

_____

_____

_____

_____

_____

_____

_____

_____

Triggers	Category

Category	Strategy

Strategy	Action

Chapter 4 Section 1 Discussion Prompts

- Share with each other your most memorable financial trauma or trigger from the past, focusing on the feelings it evoked and its impact on your current financial beliefs.

- Explore together the emotions tied to each of your financial traumas, describing any fear, anxiety, or stress associated with these moments to foster understanding.

- Reflect on how each other's financial triggers might influence your joint financial decisions, encouraging empathy and deeper insight into each other's reactions.

- Discuss the physical sensations you experience when faced with financial challenges, such as tension, racing heart, wanting to hide or avoid, and lashing out, to increase awareness and compassion for each other's stress responses.

- Envision together a future scenario where a financial trigger might arise and collaboratively brainstorm supportive actions to comfort and reassure each other during those times.

Discussion Notes

_____
_____
_____
_____
_____
_____
_____
_____
_____
_____
_____
_____
_____
_____
_____
_____
_____
_____
_____
_____

Section 2
Communication Strategies for Constructive Conversations

In this section, you will establish a shared approach to discussing finances in a way that prioritizes understanding, support, empathy, and collaborative action.

This compass will guide you through future financial conversations, making them more constructive and less stressful. It will also allow you to consider each others perspective in each decision and make it easier to build a foundation that serves everyone's needs.

Create Guidelines For All Important Discussions

As you create a plan to follow for your discussions, there are things to ensure are included but feel free to add your own additions.

Must Includes:

Where do important conversations take place and what is required by each person to feel safe and not feel attacked?

Establish ground rules. Are there any words and phrases that are off limits. Refer to the triggering section for reference.

I recommend always starting with a grounding meditation. I have provided one in the tool box.

Always allow each partner to share concerns at the very beginning. Use I statements, never placing blame on the other person.

Identify Common Ground: Together, highlight the concerns and goals you both share. Acknowledging mutual priorities can lay a foundation for understanding and cooperation.

Remember your safe word and always be mindful of approaching every conversation with love and compassion. Even when you do not agree, you are both on the same team

Crafting Connections of the Heart

Chamber of Understanding: Openly share what each of you needs to feel truly heard and understood. Whether it's through active listening, acknowledging each other's feelings, or exercising patience, pave the way to mutual comprehension.

Foundation of Support: Delve into how each partner feels most supported during discussions about finances. This could involve words of encouragement, being physically there for one another, or tackling challenges together.

Wings of Empathy: By sharing the stories and experiences that have shaped your financial views, you create wings of empathy. This understanding allows for patience and compassion in future conversations.

Pathway to Progress: Together, outline concrete steps to achieve your united financial dreams. This means setting clear responsibilities, deadlines, and celebrating each small victory on your journey.

Circle of Gratitude: Close your heart-to-heart by thanking each other for the openness and dedication shown. Recognize every step forward, no matter the size, and reaffirm your commitment to these strategies of love and understanding.

Crafting Connections of the Heart
Pathway to Progress

Action Step 1

Action Step 2

Action Step 3

Action Step 4

Chapter 4 Section 2 Discussion Prompts

- Explore together what each of you needs to feel understood and truly heard. Focus on listening actively, acknowledging emotions, and practicing patience to foster deeper understanding.

- Discuss the types of support each partner finds most comforting during financial conversations. Whether it's through encouragement, presence, or working as a team, identify how to best support each other.

- Share personal stories that have shaped your views on money. This sharing builds empathy, allowing both partners to approach financial discussions with greater patience and compassion.

- Create a plan with actionable steps towards achieving your shared financial goals. Assign responsibilities, set deadlines, and celebrate each achievement to progress together.

- End discussions with expressions of gratitude for each other's openness and commitment. Acknowledge every step forward, reinforcing your dedication to growing together with understanding and love.

Discussion Notes

Section 3
Resolving Conflicts with Compassion and Compromise

As with the previous section, this exercise is discussion-based. As you have these deep conversations and find common ground, think about ways to incorporate the pieces that give you comfort into your regular communication style.

This journal is, of course, geared toward money, but the strategies and exercises can be used for any challenging topic of conversation.

Establish the boundaries and begin the discussion

Set the stage by revisiting the guidelines you both established in the previous section, reinforcing the notion that you're allies in this journey.

Clearly define the conflict at hand. Identify the specific points of contention and where your perspectives diverge. Often, what seems like disagreement may stem from a misunderstanding of each other's viewpoints.

Recognize the shared values and aspirations you hold regarding your finances, particularly in relation to this conflict. Explore potential areas for compromise and ascertain if there are any non-negotiables that require attention.

Next, utilize the formula provided on the following page to construct a compromise. Ensure that the solution prioritizes both partners' sense of safety and validation while remaining in harmony with your overarching goals and values.

Craft a Compassionate Compromise:

With an understanding of each other's positions, brainstorm potential solutions that consider both partners' needs and concerns.

Aim for a compromise that respects both viewpoints and is aligned with your shared financial goals. Agree on actionable steps to implement this solution, and decide on how you will support each other in making these changes.

Partner 1 Requirements

Partner 2 Requirements

The Compromise:

Chapter 4 Section 3 Discussion Prompts

- Explore how both partners view compromise in their relationship. Discuss times when compromise felt like a shared victory rather than a personal loss, highlighting the importance of mutual benefit and support.

- Reflect on a situation where compromise led to unexpected positive outcomes. This encourages viewing compromise not as a sacrifice but as a creative solution that can lead to better results for both.

- Discuss each partner's biggest fears regarding compromise in financial decisions. Understanding these fears can pave the way for more empathetic and supportive negotiations.

- Share personal definitions of a successful compromise. This helps align expectations and creates a common understanding of what achieving a win-win situation looks like in the context of your relationship.

- Brainstorm scenarios that may require compromise in the future and propose hypothetical solutions. Practicing compromise in a low-stakes setting can build confidence and ease in handling real-life situations.

Discussion Notes

Chapter 5

Money Management Techniques

Section 1
Effective Saving Strategies for Couple

Embarking on the journey to financial security and wealth-building together marks a significant milestone for you as a couple. It begins with understanding your options and making choices that resonate with your shared aspirations and values.

Shifting from the habit of spending everything in your bank account and wallet is pivotal. By proactively transferring funds to savings or a money market account before expenses, you enforce a disciplined approach to expenditure. For instance, many companies offer the option to allocate a portion of your payroll directly to your savings, leaving the remainder to cover expenses and discretionary spending.

Consider earmarking a segment of your income for a savings account—a financial safety net and a stepping stone toward larger objectives. View it as the collective peace of mind silently growing amidst the hustle and bustle of daily life.

When delving into investments, broaden your perspective. From the stock market to real estate, various avenues present diverse potential rewards and risks. The crux lies in aligning your investment choices with your risk tolerance, financial objectives, and time horizon. Remember, investing is akin to a marathon, not a sprint; it's about cultivating wealth steadily over time by leveraging your resources wisely.

Prioritize retirement savings as a crucial component of investing in your collective future selves. Retirement accounts offer distinct advantages that facilitate more efficient growth of your money over the long haul.

Committing to investing a minimum of $300 per month can significantly impact your future financial well-being. Beginning this journey early enables compounding interest to work its magic, amplifying the growth potential over time.

Consider gamifying your savings to reinforce positive habits. Whenever you opt out of purchasing a luxury item like a fancy coffee or an extravagant dinner with friends, redirect the saved funds from your primary account to your savings. Celebrate these small victories, acknowledging the extra amount accumulated through minor adjustments to daily spending habits. Establish a non-negotiable rule to promptly transfer these "choosing me" funds to savings whenever you opt for long-term gratification over instant indulgence, preventing impulsive spending.

Navigating the balance between savings and investments may feel daunting, but it's about taking the first step and learning along the way. Engage in discussions about your shared vision for the future, evaluate your current financial standing, and collectively determine initial actions that resonate with both of you. This could entail opening a joint savings account, initiating a modest investment in a mutual fund, or increasing contributions to your retirement accounts. The key is to embark on this journey together, fostering financial security and prosperity for your future selves.

Remember, the most important thing is to start. You don't have to have all the answers right away. Your financial strategy will evolve as you do. The act of choosing and starting together is itself a powerful step towards building a prosperous future. Open, honest communication and a willingness to adapt are your best tools as you navigate this path side by side.

In the boxes below write 3 short term savings you want to focus on and 3 long term saving options. Once you have chosen all 6, number them in priority order.

Once you have chosen the priority, create a goal, a timeline for the goal and go add it to your budget.

Short Term Savings Focus

Long Term Savings Focus

Chapter 5 Section 1 Discussion Prompts

- Explore together how each savings option aligns with your short-term and long-term goals, discussing the benefits and limitations in relation to your shared vision for the future.

- Reflect on the level of accessibility you both desire from your savings, considering if immediate access is crucial or if you can commit to longer-term options with potentially higher yields.

- Evaluate your joint comfort level with risk, comparing traditional savings accounts with other investment vehicles, and decide which balance of security and potential growth feels right for both of you.

- Discuss how each savings option fits into your overall financial plan, including emergency funds, retirement savings, and other financial goals, to ensure a holistic approach to your finances.

- Set a regular schedule to review and adjust your savings strategies together, ensuring they continue to meet your evolving needs and goals, fostering open communication and flexibility in your financial planning.

Discussion Notes

Section 2
Smart Spending Habits

Creating smart spending habits doesn't mean squeezing every ounce of joy out of your budget or turning every purchase into a battle of wills. It's about finding a balanced approach that allows for the flexibilities of life, including those all-important moments of entertainment and joy.

When you both work together to understand and respect your financial boundaries, it's easier to enjoy spending without guilt or worry. Start by setting clear, shared goals that include savings, necessary expenses, and yes, fun money. This ensures that you're both working towards something meaningful while still honoring your need for enjoyment and relaxation.

Communication is key. Regularly discuss your spending plans, expectations, and any adjustments that might need to be made to accommodate life's ever-changing landscape. Be open about your desires and listen to each other's. Compromise is not about one winning and the other losing; it's about finding a path that respects both of your needs and desires.

Mistakes happen; they're part of the learning process. If one partner overspends, approach the situation with kindness and compassion rather than blame. Use it as an opportunity to understand what led to the overspend and how you can support each other to prevent it in the future. Remember, it's not about perfection but progress. Celebrating small victories and learning from missteps together strengthens your relationship and your financial foundation.

Allow yourselves the flexibility to enjoy life's pleasures. Whether it's a date night, a small trip, or something as simple as a favorite snack, these moments of joy are important. They remind you why you're working hard and saving in the first place. By balancing smart spending habits with life's pleasures, you honor your partnership and build a happier, more sustainable financial life together.

Start by making a list of things each partner would like to keep and things each partner would like to eliminate from the spending. Go through the entire budget, not just things you consider "discretionary" and while you likely will not eliminate non-discretionary items, this is a good time to discuss how much you spend in those other categories and evaluate opportunities,

Remember to always follow the guidelines you created in previous sections to set yourself up for success.

Once both partners have made their list, discuss what changes you will make and also highlight things you are already doing well. Make sure to update your budget with any changes.

Partner 1

Elimination / Adjustment List

_____
_____
_____
_____

Keep List

_____
_____
_____
_____

Non-Negotiables

_____
_____
_____

Partner 2

Elimination / Adjustment List

_____

_____

_____

_____

Keep List

_____

_____

_____

_____

Non-Negotiables

_____

_____

Chapter 5 Section 2 Discussion Prompts

- Explore together how your current spending aligns with your shared goals. Consider what adjustments might be needed to ensure you're both moving towards what matters most to you.

- Identify areas in your spending where you feel there's room for improvement or reduction. Discuss how these changes could impact your financial health and relationship positively.

- Share personal triggers or habits that lead to unnecessary spending. By understanding these, you can develop strategies to support each other in avoiding or managing them.

- Discuss the importance of setting aside funds for enjoyment and how you can incorporate this into your budget without compromising your financial goals. Finding a balance between saving and living is crucial.

- Agree on a regular check-in schedule to review your spending, progress towards your goals, and any adjustments needed in your approach. This keeps communication open and ensures you're both accountable and supportive of each other.

Discussion Notes

Secton 3
Investment Basics for Building Wealth Together

Exploring investment strategies can be an exciting step towards building your shared wealth as you embark on this journey together. It's essential to remember that investing is not just about the potential for financial gain; it's about making your money work for you together as you build your future.

Firstly, recognize the importance of diversity in your investments. This doesn't mean you have to dive into every option available at once. It's perfectly okay to start with one investment type and gradually expand your portfolio. This cautious approach allows you to learn as you go, reducing risk and increasing your confidence in investment decisions.

It also helps you learn more about each other, what each of you like and don't like, your individual risk aversion and overall philosophes around wealth building.

Just like everything else in this journal, use this is an opportunity to build on each of your financial strengths, provide support to each other and always discuss things with an open mind and an open heart.

Disclaimer: While I am going to give specific examples, including potential benefits to options nothing in this journal should be construed as direct financial advise, every person and couple is different and has different goals. If you want customized investment advise I recommend contacting a financial professional that can evaluate your specific circumstances and goals.

Consider initiating your investment journey with mutual funds, index funds, or ETFs. These options are particularly advantageous for beginners as they pool your funds with those of other investors to acquire a diverse range of stocks or bonds. This inherent diversification helps mitigate risk, offering a more stable introduction to the investment landscape.

As you become more adept, explore additional avenues such as individual stocks, real estate, or emerging sectors like cryptocurrency. Nothing needs to be off-limits unless mutually agreed upon; however, it's wise to conduct thorough research and seek guidance from professionals specializing in each area when necessary.

Maintain a foundation of mutual respect and collaboration in your investment decisions. Both partners' opinions and comfort levels should be honored, fostering open and honest discussions about potential investments, associated risks, and their alignment with long-term objectives.

Remember, progress is incremental, and it's perfectly acceptable to proceed at a gradual pace. Wealth accumulation is a journey, not a race. By commencing early, even with modest investments, you're laying the groundwork for a more secure financial future together. View each investment as a stride toward your collective aspirations, prioritizing kindness and empathy, especially during the inevitable fluctuations of the investment landscape.

As you begin to research options I encourage you to do so both independently and then together. Write out things that sound appealing and take into consideration things you have access to through an employer like 401ks.

If you have children or intend to have them, this is a good time to discuss if you want to set up things for them like college funds.

This is also a good time to explore and discuss life insurance. We will talk more about basic estate planning in a later chapter but this is a good time to start thinking about it.

Remember, nothing needs to be off the table. If it can help you grow your wealth you should discuss it openly and respectfully as a team.

P:artnr 1 Investment Interests

Partner 2 Investment Interests

Chapter 5 Section 3 Discussion Prompts

Discuss how each partner's personal history with money might be influencing their current views on investing. Share any fears and listen to each other with empathy.

Explore together how the stories you've heard about money from family and friends shape your attitudes towards investments. Identify if these narratives are helping or hindering your financial planning.

Talk about the emotions that come up when you think about investing your money. Are these feelings rooted in past experiences or fears about the future? How can you support each other in moving past them?

Consider the financial goals you both have and how investing can help achieve them. Delve into what kinds of investments feel right for both of you, considering your shared values and risk tolerance.

Create a space where you can openly discuss any apprehensions about investment options. Work together to research and understand different strategies, making decisions that feel comfortable and exciting for both of you.

Discussion Notes

_____
_____
_____
_____
_____
_____
_____
_____
_____
_____
_____
_____
_____
_____
_____
_____
_____
_____

Chapter 6

Routine Financial Check-Ins

Section 1
Establishing Regular Financial Check-ins

Leaning into regular financial check-ins as a couple is like nurturing the garden of your shared dreams; it requires attention, care, and occasional weeding to flourish. These check-ins are your opportunity to sit down together, review your budget, evaluate your progress towards your goals, and make necessary adjustments. Life is dynamic, and as it unfolds, your financial priorities and goals may shift. Regular reviews ensure that your financial plan remains aligned with your current realities and aspirations.

Consider these check-ins as a chance to celebrate your successes, no matter how small. Did you stick to your dining-out budget this month? Have you paid off a significant chunk of debt? Acknowledging these victories together not only reinforces positive behavior but also strengthens your bond. And practice holding space for celebrating, it's so easy to discount or say I could have done better. Honor what you did and build on your accomplishments.

Moreover, these discussions provide a safe space to address any setbacks or challenges head-on, without blame or judgment. Perhaps unexpected expenses arose, or one of you splurged a bit too freely. By approaching these issues together, you cultivate a culture of openness and support, rather than secrecy or shame. Adjusting your goals during these check-ins is not an admission of failure but a sign of flexibility and mutual support. Life throws curveballs, and what seemed important six months ago may no longer be a priority. By reassessing and realigning your goals, you ensure that your financial plans serve your current needs and aspirations, not past versions of yourselves.

In essence, these financial heart-to-hearts are less about numbers and more about nurturing your partnership and shared vision for the future. This time is an investment in your relationship's health and happiness, grounding you in a mutual commitment to support each other's dreams and navigate challenges together.

So, make a date with your budget, bring your dreams, challenges, and a spirit of teamwork, and watch your shared financial garden thrive.

Take a few minutes now to decide how you want to have this check-ins and consider the following questions.

> How often do you need to meet?
>
> Do you want to have a regularly scheduled meeting on the calendar?
>
> How can you make these check-ins fun?
>
> What do you need to prepare?
>
> Who is doing what?

Chapter 6 Section 1 Discussion Prompts

- Explore what activities or goals make you both feel most connected and excited. Discuss integrating these into your financial plan to make savings and spending align more closely with shared joys.

- Share personal victories or positive changes you've noticed in each other's financial habits. Celebrating these moments can reinforce good practices and deepen your bond.

- Suggest a fun challenge for the next month, like finding creative ways to save money together or setting a joint savings goal for something you both enjoy. Discuss strategies and track your progress together.

- Reflect on a financial fear or worry and discuss how you can support each other in overcoming it. This openness fosters trust and understanding.

- Propose a dream project or purchase and brainstorm steps to make it a reality. Planning for a shared future can be an exciting way to strengthen your partnership and make financial discussions more engaging.

Discussion Notes

Section 2
Check-In Agendas and Discussion Guides

Agenda Suggestions

To begin using the guidelines of the agenda on the next page, and take a moment to reflect individually what occurred since the last time you met and where you would like to improve on your commitment to your individual and group goals. As well as, what your intention is for this meeting.

This is another perfect time to use the QR Code.

Agenda

Opening Gratitude Moment: Begin by expressing gratitude for each other's commitment to the journey and any financial progress made since the last check-in.

Budget Review: Examine your current budget together, noting any deviations and discussing the reasons behind them.

Goal Evaluation: Revisit your financial goals, assess progress, and make necessary adjustments.

Future Planning: Identify upcoming financial obligations and opportunities, and plan how to address them as a team.

Closing with Connection: End with a positive note about your partnership and financial future.

Chapter 6 Section 2 Discussion Prompts

- Reflect on how regularly checking in on finances has influenced your relationship. Discuss ways to make these sessions more enjoyable and stress-free.

- Discuss any unexpected expenses or income from the period and how they were managed. Consider how you can better prepare for similar situations in the future.

- Share feelings and insights gained from recent financial decisions or changes. Open up about any concerns and brainstorm solutions together.

- Delve into how your individual and joint financial goals are evolving. Are there new dreams or priorities that need to be incorporated into your plans?

- Celebrate successes, no matter how small. Acknowledge each other's contributions towards your financial wellbeing and discuss how you can build on these wins moving forward.

Discussion Notes

Section 3
Celebrating Milestones and Adjusting Goals

Celebrating financial milestones together isn't just about acknowledging success; it's a powerful act of unity. It serves as a reminder of the strength found in shared goals and the victories achieved through teamwork.

Equally important is setting goals together, which fosters a deeper bond and mutual understanding. It's an opportunity to dream together and map out a future that reflects both of your aspirations.

This process of celebrating achievements and setting new objectives is crucial because it keeps you both motivated and focused, ensuring you're always moving forward together.

Embrace each moment of achievement and every step of planning as milestones in your journey, not just towards financial prosperity, but towards a stronger, more connected partnership.

Part 1: Milestone Celebration

Choose a Milestone you have recently as a couple and reflect on what it means to you in the boxes below.

Milestone Description:

Partner 1 Reflection:

Partner 2 Reflection:

Part 2: Goal Evaluation and Adjustment

Take the time right now to evaluate every goal you have made as a couple throughout this process and write them out in a list with status and timeline. Take a moment to celebrate every completed goal and the steps you have taken towards everything that is currently in progress.

Be sure to add any adjustments to your goal tracker and/or budget it appropriate.

Goal	Status	Notes / Adjustments

Part 3: Create an Action Plan

Use the following pages to write out an action plan for anything that you were inspired to change or add to your goal list. When you have fully written it out, be sure to update your goal tracker and budget!

_____

_____

_____

_____

_____

_____

_____

_____

_____

_____

_____

_____

_____

_____

_____

Chapter 6 Section 3 Discussion Prompts

- Explore together the smallest financial milestones you've achieved recently. How do these small victories align with your larger goals and what do they mean for your journey together?

- Share your feelings about the importance of recognizing every financial achievement, no matter its size. Discuss how this practice can reinforce your bond and commitment to your shared financial future.

- Reflect on a recent small financial milestone. What steps did you both take to reach it, and how can you replicate this success for future goals?

- Imagine a celebration that honors both your individual contributions and your achievements as a couple. What elements would make this celebration meaningful and reflective of your journey together?

- Discuss the impact of celebrating small wins on your motivation and outlook towards financial planning. How can this practice help maintain your momentum and keep you both engaged in the process?

Discussion Notes

Chapter 7

Building Wealth Beyond Bank Accounts

Section 1
Investing in Each Other's Dreams and Passions

Investing in each other's dreams and passions from the start of a relationship lays the foundation for a wealth that transcends financial statements. This practice is about recognizing and nurturing the intangible assets of love, support, and shared vision that enrich a partnership beyond measure.

When couples actively support each other's aspirations, they cultivate an environment of mutual respect and encouragement. This nurturing space allows each individual to grow, explore, and reach their full potential. Such support can manifest in various forms—be it through time, words of encouragement, or shared resources—and it signals to each other that their dreams matter. This collective belief in one another's goals reinforces the bond between partners, making the relationship itself a source of immeasurable wealth.

Investing in dreams and passions also opens up new avenues for financial prosperity. When individuals feel supported, they are more likely to take calculated risks, pursue innovative ideas, and seek opportunities that align with their passions. These endeavors not only contribute to personal fulfillment but can also lead to financial gain and diversification of income sources.

Moreover, this practice strengthens the couple's ability to work as a team. By aligning their efforts towards common goals and supporting each other's individual pursuits, partners develop a deeper understanding of collaborative planning and decision-making. This skill is invaluable in navigating the financial aspects of their life together, from budgeting and saving to investing and wealth building.

Starting this practice early in the relationship establishes a strong foundation for future financial planning. It ensures that both partners' dreams and goals are woven into the fabric of their joint financial strategy, making the pursuit of financial goals a more fulfilling and unified endeavor.

Ultimately, investing in each other's dreams and passions underscores the principle that the true value of wealth lies not in the balance of a bank account, but in the richness of the life shared together. It's a reminder that while financial wealth is important, the wealth created through love, support, and shared dreams is priceless.

Ideas

- Weekly dream discussions
- Share career goals
- Attend workshops together
- Budget for hobbies
- Joint business venture
- Support artistic endeavors
- Plan travel adventures
- Encourage further education
- Celebrate small victories
- Seek mutual interests
- Art supplies purchase
- Course enrollments
- Joint investment account
- Startup funding support
- Home studio setup
- Travel savings fund
- Book publication costs
- Music production gear
- Fitness equipment
- Language class fees

List a few of your own... _____

_____

_____

Chapter 7 Section 1 Discussion Prompts

- Discuss what dreams and passions each of you holds dear. How can you both contribute to making these a reality, considering time, energy, and resources?

- Explore how investing in each other's dreams can strengthen your bond. What are the ways you can support each other without necessarily making a financial commitment?

- Consider the financial aspect of supporting each other's ambitions. What adjustments could you make to your budget to accommodate these investments?

- Reflect on the long-term impact of nurturing each other's dreams. How do you think this mutual support will affect your relationship and individual fulfillment over time?

- Create a plan of action. After identifying how you can support each other's dreams, both financially and otherwise, outline the first few steps you will take together to start this journey.

Discussion Notes

Section 2
Philanthropy and Giving Back Together

Philanthropy isn't just about writing checks to worthy causes; it's a powerful expression of your shared values and vision as a couple. When you give back together, you're not only contributing to the greater good, but you're also fortifying your bond, aligning your goals, and solidifying the foundation upon which your relationship stands. This joint act of generosity serves as a testament to your commitment to not just each other, but to the world around you.

Embarking on a philanthropic journey together encourages dialogue about what matters most to each of you, fostering deeper understanding and respect. It opens up conversations about your beliefs, your passions, and the legacy you want to leave behind. These discussions are invaluable, as they allow you to discover common ground and perhaps even inspire new shared interests.

Moreover, giving back is a reminder of your collective power to effect change. It underscores the principle that, together, you are more than the sum of your parts. This realization can be incredibly empowering, reinforcing your partnership's strength and the positive impact you can have on the world.

Incorporating philanthropy into your lives is also a practical way to instill joint core values, especially if you plan to grow your family. It sets a precedent of kindness, generosity, and social responsibility for future generations.

As you embark on this fulfilling path, take the time to pick a cause that resonates with both of you deeply. Discuss and decide on a dollar amount that feels meaningful yet responsible, considering your financial goals and budget. Making this commitment not only amplifies your impact on the cause you care about but also reinforces your commitment to each other and the values you share.

So, take that step today. Choose a cause that aligns with your joint values, decide on a contribution that fits your budget, and weave this act of giving into the tapestry of your life together. It's a decision that will enrich your relationship and the world around you.

Your Cause:

Dollar Amount and Frequency:

Chapter 7 Section 2 Discussion Prompts

- Discuss the causes that ignite your passion and why they matter to both of you, highlighting the joy of finding shared meaning in giving back.

- Explore the feelings and experiences you hope to gain by supporting these causes together, focusing on the emotional rewards and deeper connection.

- Share stories or moments when giving back made a significant impact on your lives individually, then envision the amplified effect of doing it as a united front.

- Brainstorm creative ways to contribute to your chosen cause beyond financial donations, like volunteering time or using your skills, to keep your philanthropic efforts engaging and varied.

- Reflect on how supporting these causes aligns with your shared values and how this joint effort enhances your relationship, emphasizing the growth and enrichment it brings to your bond.

Discussion Notes

Section 3
Planning for the Future: Estate Planning, Insurance, and Legacy Building

There are more specific estate planning resources at the QR code below.

Young couples often focus on the present, embracing the joys and challenges that come with building a life. However, an equally important aspect of this journey is planning for the future.

This involves not just dreaming about what you want to achieve but also preparing for the unforeseen and ensuring a secure legacy for yourselves and your loved ones. Let's explore the essentials of estate planning, insurance, and legacy building, and why they're crucial for young couples.

Estate planning might seem daunting or even unnecessary early in your relationship, especially if you are young. However, it's about more than just distributing assets; it's about making decisions that affect your partnership and any future family members.

It involves legally documenting your wishes regarding asset distribution, care of minor children, and decisions about health care should you be unable to make them yourselves. Estate planning ensures that your wishes are honored and your loved ones are cared for, according to your desires, not a court's decision.

Insurance is another pillar of future planning, offering protection against life's uncertainties. Health, life, and disability insurance safeguard your most valuable asset—your ability to earn. In the face of illness, injury, or worse, insurance can provide financial stability, allowing you to focus on what truly matters—each other's well-being and future goals.

Lastly, legacy building transcends financial wealth; it's about the values, lessons, and memories you leave behind. It involves creating a positive impact that outlives you, whether through philanthropy, business, or simply the way you lead your lives. By starting to think about your legacy early, you can make intentional choices that align with how you want to be remembered.

For young couples, the journey ahead is both exciting and unpredictable. By incorporating estate planning, insurance, and a vision for your legacy into your early planning, you not only protect each other but also lay the foundation for a future that reflects your shared values and dreams. This proactive approach ensures that you're prepared for whatever life throws your way, allowing you to focus on building a life together that's as secure as it is fulfilling.

Options to Consider

- Create a joint will
- Appoint durable powers of attorney
- Establish healthcare directives
- Discuss guardianship wishes
- Open joint savings accounts
- Purchase life insurance policies
- Plan charitable giving strategies
- Document digital asset wishes
- Review beneficiaries regularly
- Schedule annual financial reviews
- Set up trust funds
- Consider long-term care insurance
- Identify financial goals together
- Discuss retirement plans and accounts
- Explore tax implications and strategies
- Craft a comprehensive budget plan
- Secure property and asset titles
- Share financial knowledge and resources
- Plan for children's education funds
- Cultivate a shared investment strategy

Estate and legacy planning doesn't require completing every task immediately. Choose three from this list or from your own research that feel most important to both of you.

Incorporate these into your goals tracker and timeline, making manageable steps towards your future together.

Chapter 7 Section 3 Discussion Prompts

- Imagine your ideal legacy. What values and contributions do you want to leave behind, and how can you start building that together now?

- Discuss how you envision your estate supporting your loved ones and causes dear to you. What steps can you take today to make this vision a reality?

- Consider the impact of your financial decisions on future generations. How can you ensure that your choices today contribute positively to their lives?

- Explore the concept of philanthropy in your legacy planning. What causes are most important to both of you, and how can you integrate support for them into your financial plans?

- Reflect on the memories and values you wish to pass on. How can you use your estate and legacy planning to ensure these are preserved and cherished by future generations?

Discussion Notes

_____
_____
_____
_____
_____
_____
_____
_____
_____
_____
_____
_____
_____
_____
_____
_____
_____
_____

Chapter 8

Maintaining Financial Wellness

Section 1
Continuous Learning and Growth in Financial Knowledge

Learning and growing together in financial knowledge is a cornerstone for couples aiming to build a lasting and harmonious relationship. As your lives and goals intertwine, so too should your understanding of how to navigate the financial world together. This shared journey of financial education is not just about managing your money better; it's about deepening your bond through common goals and shared experiences.

As you explore financial concepts together, you will develop a shared language that makes discussing money matters, from daily spending to long-term planning, both easier and more effective. Engaging in this learning process together means both partners have an equal stake and say in financial decisions. It eliminates imbalances and misunderstandings that can lead to conflict, fostering a partnership based on mutual respect and shared knowledge.

This commitment to financial literacy empowers you to make informed decisions, whether it's about investments, savings, or major purchases. Understanding the risks and opportunities of financial decisions enables you to navigate life's uncertainties with confidence, together. It also ensures both partners can capably manage the household finances, providing peace of mind and security.

Keeping pace with the evolving economic landscape is essential. The financial world is never static, and staying informed helps you adapt your strategies to meet your changing needs and goals. This adaptability is crucial for seizing new opportunities and safeguarding against unforeseen challenges.

Engaging in continuous financial learning is a testament to your commitment to each other and your shared future. It's about more than just financial prosperity; it's about building a partnership that's resilient, informed, and united in facing whatever the future holds. Together, you're not just planning for your financial future; you're investing in the strength and depth of your relationship, crafting a legacy of knowledge, security, and mutual support.

Charting Our Learning Journey Together

Objective: This exercise aims to help couples identify and prioritize three financial topics they wish to explore together, fostering mutual growth and understanding in their financial journey.

Brainstorming Session:

Each partner writes down financial topics or questions they're curious about or feel they need to understand better. This could range from investment strategies, retirement planning, insurance options, to budgeting techniques.

Sharing Insights:

Take turns sharing your list with each other. Explain why each topic interests you or why you feel it's important to learn about it.

Finding Common Ground:

Discuss the topics each of you has brought to the table and identify any common interests or areas where one partner's interest sparks curiosity in the other.

Highlight the topics that you both feel are most relevant to your current financial situation or future goals.

Prioritizing Together:

From your shared list of interests, work together to choose three topics that you both agree to explore further.

Consider what information or skills you hope to gain and how learning about these topics could benefit your relationship and financial future.

Making a Decision

For each chosen topic, decide on a specific action or learning activity you will undertake. This could be reading a book, attending a workshop, or scheduling consultations with financial advisors.
Set a timeline for when you wish to start and complete your learning activities for each topic.

Partner 1 *Partner 2*

Chosen Topics

Chapter 8 Section 1 Discussion Prompts

- Reflect on one financial topic you've always been curious about and discuss why it interests you.

- Consider how jointly learning about a specific financial area could reinforce both our relationship and our future security.

- Identify a financial skill that, if developed together, could significantly benefit our shared life. Explore why it stands out to you.

- Talk about any financial concerns or uncertainties that could be alleviated by gaining knowledge in a particular area.

- Brainstorm engaging and enjoyable methods to explore these financial subjects together, making the learning process a shared adventure.

Discussion Notes

Section 2
Keeping the Spark Alive: Fun and Creative Money Dates

Keeping the spark alive in a relationship often revolves around finding new, exciting experiences to share. When it comes to managing finances together, this principle still applies. Introducing fun and creative money dates can transform seemingly mundane tasks like budgeting or financial planning into moments of connection and joy.

By dedicating time to focus on your financial health in a playful and engaging setting, you not only strengthen your financial foundation but also deepen your bond.

These special dates create a space for open communication, shared dreams, and collective goal-setting, all while enjoying each other's company.

Here are five date suggestions to keep the financial spark alive:

1. Budgeting picnic in the park
2. Dream planning at a cozy café
3. Investment research over homemade dinner
4. Savings goals brainstorm at a scenic lookout
5. Financial book club for two with your favorite snacks

Take a few minutes now and Plan and Schedule your first date!

Chapter 8 Section 2 Discussion Prompts

- Discuss what aspect of your finances you're both curious about exploring together. It could be investments, savings strategies, or learning about each other's spending habits.

- Share one financial goal you each have and think about how a date can be designed around planning to achieve these goals together.

- Reflect on a financial topic you've found challenging or intimidating. Consider using a date to tackle this topic in a supportive and relaxed setting.

- Brainstorm activities that both of you find enjoyable and see how you can incorporate a financial planning element into them. For example, if you love hiking, could you discuss your dream of buying a home while on a trail?

- Talk about a financial success story from each of your lives. Plan a date to celebrate these successes and discuss how you can build more together.

Discussion Notes

Section 3
When to Seek Professional Financial Advice

Seeking professional financial advice is a crucial step for couples who are navigating the complex landscape of financial planning. It not only ensures that you're making informed decisions but also provides a safety net for your financial future.

Expert guidance can help identify opportunities you might have overlooked and avoid common pitfalls. It's particularly beneficial during significant life changes or when making decisions that have long-term implications on your wealth and security.

Examples where it's important to seek professional financial advice include:

- Planning for retirement to ensure you have a comfortable and secure future.
- Investing in stocks, bonds, or other investment vehicles to grow your wealth.
- Buying or selling real estate to make sure it aligns with your financial goals.
- Estate planning to ensure your assets are distributed according to your wishes.
- Navigating tax planning to minimize liabilities and maximize returns.
- Managing debt, especially if it's becoming unmanageable or affecting your financial goals.
- Considering a large financial gift or inheritance to understand its impact on your finances.
- Starting a business or investing in one, to assess the financial viability and risks involved.

Chapter 8 Section 3 Discussion Prompts

- Explore together what financial challenges or goals you feel are beyond your current knowledge. Is there a specific area where you feel stuck or unsure?

- Discuss any major life changes or financial decisions on the horizon. How comfortable do you both feel navigating these changes without professional input?

- Reflect on your long-term financial goals. Do you feel confident in your current plan to achieve them, or would external advice give you more peace of mind?

- Consider your experiences with financial planning so far. Have there been moments when you wished for expert guidance to avoid mistakes or maximize opportunities?

- Talk about your financial health as a couple. Where do you see the value in investing in professional financial advice to ensure a secure and prosperous future together?

Discussion Notes

The Toolbox

This journal was built for you to be able to develop a routine, sit down together and do many of the exercises and prompts right in the book.

In addition to everything in the journal, there are a vast number of additional resources on the QR code including budgeting spreadsheets, additional meditations, videos and ways to connect with me directly.

The Toolbox

Monthly Budget

SOURCE OF INCOME	AMOUNT
TOTAL INCOME	

MONTH OF:

MY GOALS
○
○
○
○

PAYABLE BILL	DUE DATE	AMOUNT	PAID	NOTES

TOTAL INCOME	TOTAL EXPENSES	DIFFERENCE

The Toolbox

Monthly Budget Planner

Add in baby cost - see QR code for one-off cost versus monthly additional expenses.

Budget Goal:_____   Month:_____

Income

Date	Description	Amount
Total		

Fixed Expenses

Date	Description	Amount
Total		

Other Expenses

Date	Description	Amount
Total		

Bills

Date	Description	Amount
Total		

Recap

	Goal	Actual	Difference
Earnt			
Spent			
Debt			
Saved			

The Toolbox

Big Purchase Add-on

What additional income can you bring in, or areas that you can save in and reallocate the funds to the big purchase saving's account.

WHAT % OF INCOME	AMOUNT
TOTAL INCOME	

MONTH OF:

MY GOALS
○
○
○
○

PAYABLE BILL	DUE DATE	AMOUNT	PAID	NOTES

TOTAL INCOME	TOTAL EXPENSES	DIFFERENCE

The Toolbox

Travel Budget Planner

DESTINATION	

TRANSPORTATION		
expenses	budget	actual
Total:		

ACCOMMODATION		
expenses	budget	actual
Total:		

FOOD & DRINK		
expenses	budget	actual
Total:		

TRAVEL DATES	

ACTIVITIES		
expenses	budget	actual
Total:		

PRE-TRIP EXPENSES		
expenses	budget	actual
Total:		

OTHER		
expenses	budget	actual
Total:		

The Toolbox

Reflection Pages

Additional Reflection Pages

Additional Reflection Pages

Additional Reflection Pages

Additional Reflection Pages

Additional Reflection Pages

Additional Reflection Pages

Additional Reflection Pages

Additional Reflection Pages

Additional Reflection Pages

Additional Reflection Pages

Additional Reflection Pages

Additional Reflection Pages

Additional Reflection Pages

Additional Reflection Pages

Additional Reflection Pages

Additional Reflection Pages

Additional Reflection Pages

Additional Reflection Pages

Additional Reflection Pages

Additional Reflection Pages

Additional Reflection Pages

Additional Reflection Pages

Additional Reflection Pages

Additional Reflection Pages

www.ingramcontent.com/pod-product-compliance
Lightning Source LLC
Chambersburg PA
CBHW062023050526
44107CB00106B/970